Cornerstones of Freedom

The Story of
ARLINGTON
NATIONAL
CEMETERY

By R. Conrad Stein

Illustrated by Richard Wahl

 CHILDRENS PRESS, CHICAGO

Library of Congress Cataloging in Publication Data

Stein, R   Conrad.
  The story of Arlington National Cemetery.

  (Cornerstones of freedom)
  SUMMARY: A brief history of Arlington National
Cemetery describing some of the famous and less well-
known people buried there.
  1. Arlington, Va. National Cemetery—Juvenile
literature. [1. Arlington, Va. National Cemetery]
I. Wahl, Richard, 1939-   II. Title.
F234.A7S73   975.5'295   79-14350
ISBN 0-516-04610-1

It is nine in the morning and a bus rolls over the Memorial Bridge to the Arlington National Cemetery in Virginia. Behind the bus rises the Lincoln Memorial where the huge statue of Lincoln broods over Washington, D.C. Under the bridge the waters of the Potomac flow peacefully.

The bus stops at the visitors' gate. The tourists, most of them children, crowd out. Last to leave is an old man. He slowly, almost painfully, climbs down the steps of the bus.

The tourists flock uphill to the famous landmarks—the splendid Custis-Lee Mansion, the eternal flame that burns over the grave of President John F. Kennedy, and the Tomb of the Unknown Soldier. The old man will see those places later. He takes a different path. He knows exactly where he wants to go.

The old man walks alongside a street called Pershing Drive. It cuts between long rows of white grave markers. The markers look like ranks of soldiers standing at attention. Flags of the cemetery are at half mast. It is a week day, and there is almost always a funeral at Arlington during the week. In the distance he hears a lonely bugle sounding "Taps." There are few visitors in this corner of Arlington.

He turns and walks between two rows of graves. The freshly cut grass feels like a rug under his feet. He comes to one grave and stops. The name on the stone is unimportant. He remembers only the fuzzy image of a big red-headed farm boy from Indiana. He walks past a dozen more graves and stops again. Here he remembers a tough kid who grew up on the

West Side of Chicago. The old man was friends with them both. They once huddled together in the trenches in faraway France while enemy shells exploded around them. The date on both markers is 1918.

Arlington Cemetery is often called a resting-place for heroes, but the two boys the old man knew weren't really heroes. They never won any medals. They were soldiers, like himself, following orders.

Years ago, anyone who had served with honor in the armed forces of the United States could be buried at Arlington. Now remaining grave sites are few. Permission is needed for burial there.

Too many wars, the old man thinks. Too many wars produce too many veterans to be buried at Arlington.

Not far from the graves of the old man's friends rests their commander, John J. Pershing. He was born in the backwoods of Missouri. Pershing entered West Point, graduated, and joined the cavalry. As he rose in rank to general, his critics called him arrogant and stuffy. Many said he was unable to talk to his men. But he led the American Expedition Force that went to Europe during World War I. General Pershing now lies with his men at Arlington. At his request his grave is marked by a simple GI stone.

The old man turns toward the center of the Arlington National Cemetery. He will return later to a newer section. Now he is following a route he has taken hundreds of times before. World War I was called "the war to end all wars." But history cheated the soldiers who fought it. Their sons and daughters had still more wars to fight. Elsewhere in Arlington the old man has more friends.

His walk toward the center of Arlington is a walk through American history. On a hill that rises above all else sits the Custis-Lee Mansion, or, as it is often called, the Arlington House. The more than one thousand acres that are now the Arlington National Cemetery were first bought by a Virginian named John Custis. The land had been suggested by Mr. Custis' stepfather, George Washington.

John Custis died before he could build a house on the land, and George Washington adopted his two younger children. The boy, George Washington Parke Custis, grew to adore the general. Custis was only eighteen when George Washington died. He planned to build a huge home on his land and call it Mount Washington. Later he called it Arlington after another Virginia farm owned by the Custis family. But he remained determined to dedicate his house to George Washington, the man he always considered to be his grandfather.

Custis built a graceful mansion on the top of the hill. It looked down on the new capital of the United States. His house held all of the possessions of George Washington he could collect, even the tent the General slept in while in the field.

The land around the house was cleared. Soon it became a productive farm. Custis married and had four children, but only one lived beyond a year. She was the bright and lively Mary Anna Randolph Custis. She had a childhood playmate named Robert

General Robert E. Lee

E. Lee. Lee would later become her husband and one of America's most famous generals.

Lee was already in the army when he married Mary Custis. Although his work took the couple to many parts of the United States they always loved Arlington. They considered it to be their only home. Lee was living at Arlington in April of 1861 when Fort Sumter was fired on and the United States exploded into a bitter Civil War.

Slavery was the major cause of the Civil War. Lee left no doubt where he stood on that issue. He had long ago freed the slaves he had inherited. He once wrote: "Slavery is a moral and political evil in any society, a greater evil to the white man than to the black." But Lee's loyalties remained with his native Virginia. One night he left Arlington to take command of the Armies of the South. He would never again return to the home he loved.

During the war the house and its grounds became a camp for Union soldiers. As soldiers died they were buried near the house. Later the victorious forces of the North turned the Arlington estate into a National Cemetery.

A rabbit skips across the path where the old man walks. It stops and stares at him for a moment, then scurries away. It has been a long climb, but the old man has finally reached the Custis-Lee Mansion.

He knows the history of Arlington better than almost any man alive. As the Civil War drew to a close, Lincoln was killed by an assassin, and the South lost its greatest friend. Power shifted now to the revenge-seekers in Congress. They wanted not to restore the Union, but to punish the South. How different from Lincoln's idea. He wanted to end the war, "with malice toward none, with charity toward all."

Confederate soldiers were buried at Arlington also. But bitter feelings created by the war caused Arlington to be thought of as a place where only Union soldiers ought to be buried. One day shortly after the Civil War a group of Union women went to Arlington to decorate graves. Another group of Confederate women asked to decorate the graves of their men also. They were refused. It is said that during that night a strange wind whirled about Arlington. In the morning the newly decorated Union graves were barren of flowers. The flowers had all blown over to the Confederate side.

It was at least twenty years before Confederates were freely allowed to be buried at Arlington. By then the members of Congress were mostly ex-Union soldiers. They remembered when they were soldiers. They held no hatred for their old foes.

The crowds are large at the Custis-Lee Mansion. The old man decides not to go inside. He has seen the mansion many times. He knows it has been carefully restored to look almost exactly as it did when Robert E. Lee, Mary Custis, and their children lived there.

The old man sits on the steps on the front portico. He gazes down at the city of Washington. The house behind him is rich in history. Before the Civil War the greatest names in United States history visited or dined here: Andrew Jackson, Sam Houston, Daniel Webster, and General Lafayette, to name just a few. A more recent visitor was President John F. Kennedy. He remarked how peaceful the old house was. Someone overheard him say, "I could stay here forever."

Sam Houston

Andrew Jackson

General Lafayette

Daniel Webster

Just below the Custis-Lee Mansion John Kennedy lies, resting at Arlington.

How well the old man remembers the day the young president was killed by an assassin's bullet. His sudden death shocked the nation and the world.

But the old man likes to think of Kennedy in the way he started his presidency rather than how he

John F. Kennedy

Robert Kennedy

ended it. Kennedy had been a hero in World War II
and he represented a generation that had seen
enough of war. He looked upon his presidency as a
great opportunity. He said in his inaugural address,
"The energy, the faith, the devotion which we bring

to this endeavor will light our country and all who serve it, and the glow from that fire can truly light the world." It is no wonder, the old man thinks, that his grave is symbolized by an eternal flame.

Long lines wait to pass by the Kennedy grave. After the people pay their respects, they stop at another grave marked by a simple white cross. Here lies Robert Kennedy, the president's brother. He might have become president himself had he not also been shot by an assassin. The Kennedy brothers now lie side by side, resting at Arlington.

The old man stands and takes one last look at the city of Washington. It is a beautiful city. It is the only major American city that was planned from the time it was carved out of the marshlands created by the Potomac River. Pierre L'Enfant was the young French architect who planned this city. L'Enfant now rests at Arlington near the Custis-Lee Mansion. His grave affords him a splendid view of the city he designed.

In the city the Washington Monument stands tall on the west end of the tree-shaded mall. Simple and clean, its mirror image shines up from the long reflecting pool. It was designed by an army engineer, Major General Horatio Wright, who fought in the Civil War. From his grave at Arlington, the Washington Monument can be seen towering over the city.

The old man walks on. The sun burns high above him.

To his right is the grave of Abner Doubleday, who is known as the founder of baseball. Actually, games similar to baseball had been played in the United States long before the Civil War. But Doubleday gave the game its rules and drew dimensions for the basepaths. Doubleday was also a major general in the army. His guns returned the first shots fired on Fort Sumter by the Confederates. It is said that he used baseball to keep his off-duty troops out of trouble.

The old man passes many familiar names. Eleven-year-old Johnny Clem went into the Army during the Civil War and became known as the "drummer boy of Chickamauga." He stayed in the army, became a general, and now rests at Arlington.

The first air death in the American army occurred at nearby Fort Myer. In 1908, Orville Wright was testing his new aircraft when Lieutenant Thomas Selfridge asked permission to ride as an observer. Permission was granted. After a smooth

Virgil Grissom   Edward White   Roger Chaffee

take-off, the plane suddenly plunged to the ground. Wright was injured and Selfridge killed. Lieutenant Selfridge was buried at Arlington. The Selfridge Gate of the cemetery is named in his honor.

Two of the first space casualties are also buried at Arlington. All the nation mourned when three brave astronauts, Virgil Grissom, Edward White, and

Roger Chaffee died. They were killed in an explosion and a fire while testing a spacecraft in 1967. White was buried at West Point while Grissom and Chaffee rest at Arlington. These three men made up the crew of Apollo I. Now their names also lie in the dust of the moon. The shoulder patch of the Apollo I mission was placed on the surface of the moon by the crew of Apollo XI. Alongside is the plaque that reads, "We came in peace for all mankind."

Not far from where the old man walks there is a white marble statue of a woman. She looks out at the graves of hundreds of women who once served as army and navy nurses.

The old man stops at the grave of his favorite figure in American history—Oliver Wendell Holmes. He was a man not given to blindly following orders. He became a justice on the Supreme Court and was known as the "great dissenter." He protected the rights of free speech and a free press in a manner that would have made Thomas Jefferson proud.

Holmes, son of a Boston doctor and famous poet, enlisted in the Union Army at nineteen. He had risen to the rank of captain when his unit was ordered to defend the capital against a Confederate force assembling near Fort Stevens. A pitched battle erupted. And this battle had a highly distinguished observer.

President Abraham Lincoln stood on some high ground near the fort. Captain Oliver Wendell Holmes was standing nearby. Bullets sprayed about them. The general with Lincoln said, "Mr. President, you had better move away from the firing." But Lincoln, who stood a head taller than the general, stared at the action, awed at seeing his first battle. "Mr. President, this is very dangerous," the general persisted. A soldier standing so close to Lincoln he could have touched him fell with a bullet wound. Suddenly a loud voice rang out, "Get down, you fool!" Lincoln ducked. A bullet whistled over the spot where he had just stood. The man with the

loud voice was Captain Oliver Wendell Holmes. After Lincoln brushed himself off, he turned to Holmes and said, "Young man, I'm glad you know how to talk to a civilian."

The old man smiles and walks on toward the most famous landmark in the Arlington National Cemetery. He passes a white marble amphitheater designed after those in ancient Greece. Near the amphitheater is the Tomb of the Unknown Soldier. The inscription on the tomb reads: HERE RESTS IN HONORED GLORY AN AMERICAN SOLDIER KNOWN BUT TO GOD.

Almost every war produces unknown soldiers. Men whose bodies are so mangled that identification is impossible. There were many unknown soldiers in World War I. So, in 1921, the body of an American unknown was taken from a grave in France and put to his final resting-place in the tomb at Arlington. The unknown soldier, being no one, could be anyone. So the families who lost a father, a son, a husband, or a brother could come to Arlington to pay their respects to this unknown who represents all unknowns.

The old man watches a smartly dressed young soldier marching slowly, back and forth, back and

forth, in front of the Tomb of the Unknown Soldier. The tomb is guarded day and night every day of the year.

There are now three unknown soldiers buried here. On Memorial Day of 1958, in a service led by President Eisenhower, one unknown soldier of World War II and one of the Korean War were buried at the shrine. All three rest side by side at the Tomb of the Unknown Soldier.

The recent, tragic Vietnam war produced no unknown soldiers. Medical identification has improved so much that every body recovered in that war has been identified. It is ironic, the old man thinks. Science can identify everyone killed in a war, but science can do nothing to stop the wars which produce the bodies to be buried at Arlington.

Elsewhere in Arlington lies a fallen soldier from the war in Vietnam. Lieutenant Colonel Levi Howard was a black man who grew up in Chicago. He was a star athlete in college, and after graduation became a career officer. He was that rare type

Audie Murphy

of infantry commander who was adored by his men. He was killed in Vietnam in 1969 when his helicopter was shot down. He lies now near his father, who was a corporal in World War I.

The old man returns to a section just behind where he was this morning. His walk takes him near the grave of Audie Murphy, the most decorated hero of World War II. Murphy won many decorations, including the highest honor the nation can give, the Congressional Medal of Honor. Audie Murphy was killed in a civilian plane crash in 1971, and he now rests at Arlington.

The old man now visits his friends from World War II. He fought in this war, too. He left his job as a machinist to enlist as a private just days after Pearl Harbor. He was called "Pops" then because he was old enough to be the father of many of the other privates. He has outlived a lot of them, and now many rest at Arlington.

He passes the grave of Ira H. Hayes. A bronze statue of Hayes stands just outside the cemetery overlooking the Potomac River. He was one of the Marines who raised the flag on the top of Mount Suribachi on Iwo Jima. The picture taken of this act became the most famous photograph of World War II. It also inspired the sculpture that was dedicated in 1954.

Hayes, a shy Indian from the West, became an overnight hero. His sudden fame was more than he could handle. He began drinking and died an alcoholic in 1955. Books and films have told this tragic story.

The old man reaches his friends from World War II. Again he remembers faces—the Irishman from New York, the cowboy from Texas. He remembers a noisy teenager from California who used to tease him because of his age, but who asked his help in private.

Carefully the old man sits down. The sun is edging toward the shade trees in the west. All about him are ranks of white stones, neatly lined up. Beyond him are newer graves from the Korean War. Still farther away are graves from the war in Vietnam, a war which divided the United States almost as severely as the great Civil War.

Too many wars, the old man thinks. Too many soldiers to be buried here at Arlington.

When he is alone with his friends at Arlington he always recites a line of his favorite poem. The poem is called *Dover Beach* written by Matthew Arnold:

"And we are here as on a darkling plain
Swept with confused alarms of struggle and
flight,
Where ignorant armies clash by night."

With the aid of his cane the old man climbs to his feet. He buttons his topcoat, for the afternoon air is cool. He walks slowly back to the entrance of the Arlington National Cemetery. He is tired after his long day, but he will return again—soon.

ABOUT THE AUTHOR

Mr. Stein was born in Chicago, and attended the University of Illinois where he graduated with a degree in history in 1964. He now lives in the town of San Miguel de Allende, Mexico where he is an active writer of books for young people.

To research this book Mr. Stein went to Washington, D.C. and visited the Arlington National Cemetery. He wishes to thank the many employees at Arlington whose cooperation helped him to write this book. One morning while roaming the grounds at Arlington, Mr. Stein saw another visitor—a very old man who was walking alone.

ABOUT THE ARTIST

Richard Wahl, graduate of the Art Center College of Design in Los Angeles, has illustrated a number of magazine articles and booklets. He is a skilled artist and photographer who advocates realistic interpretations of his subjects. He lives with his wife and sons in Libertyville, Illinois.